MAY   2017

The Polite Knight

Jan Westberg

Consulting Editor, Diane Craig, M.A./Reading Specialist

ABDO
Publishing Company

Published by ABDO Publishing Company, 4940 Viking Drive, Edina, Minnesota 55435.

Copyright © 2005 by Abdo Consulting Group, Inc. International copyrights reserved in all countries. No part of this book may be reproduced in any form without written permission from the publisher. SandCastle™ is a trademark and logo of ABDO Publishing Company.

Printed in the United States.

Credits
Edited by: Pam Price
Curriculum Coordinator: Nancy Tuminelly
Cover and Interior Design and Production: Mighty Media
Photo and Illustration Credits: BananaStock Ltd., Brand X Pictures, Corbis Images, Eyewire Images, Image 100, Image Source, Tracy Kompelien, PhotoDisc, Stockbyte

Library of Congress Cataloging-in-Publication Data

Westberg, Jan.
     The polite knight / Jan Westberg.
        p. cm. -- (Rhyme time)
     Includes index.
     ISBN 1-59197-812-2 (hardcover)
     ISBN 1-59197-918-8 (paperback)
     1. English language--Rhyme--Juvenile literature. I. Title. II. Rhyme time (ABDO Publishing Company)

PE1517.W48 2004
428.1'3--dc22
                                                                        2004050422

SandCastle™ books are created by a professional team of educators, reading specialists, and content developers around five essential components that include phonemic awareness, phonics, vocabulary, text comprehension, and fluency. All books are written, reviewed, and leveled for guided reading, early intervention reading, and Accelerated Reader® programs and designed for use in shared, guided, and independent reading and writing activities to support a balanced approach to literacy instruction.

Let Us Know

After reading the book, SandCastle would like you to tell us your stories about reading. What is your favorite page? Was there something hard that you needed help with? Share the ups and downs of learning to read. We want to hear from you! To get posted on the ABDO Publishing Company Web site, send us e-mail at:

sandcastle@abdopub.com

SandCastle Level: Fluent

Words that rhyme do
not have to be spelled the
same. These words rhyme
with each other:

appetite

might

campsite

polite

flight

recite

knight

right

invite

sight

Kylie is sitting on a **flight** of stairs.

When it comes to sandwiches,
Jeff has a big appetite.

Lanie is playing chess.

She could take a pawn with her **knight**.

Sally enjoys playing at her family's **campsite**.

When the pitch comes, Raymond will swing with all his **might**.

Macy gets to **invite** all of her friends to her birthday party.

Jay practices writing the alphabet until he gets all of the letters right.

Alicia is sticking out her tongue.

Making faces at others is not very **polite**.

Breanna wears glasses because she has poor **sight**.

Gordon is writing a poem that he will **recite** in class.

The Polite Knight

Sir Henry was a very brave knight.

Sometimes he rode left,
sometimes he rode right.

But wherever he went,
he was always polite.

Trusty Steed,
please go right.

15

When they saw the knight,
some birds took flight.

One night he came to a small campsite.

The people there were quite a sight.

They invited him to have a bite.

Come have a bite.

"My long ride has given me an appetite.

I thank you for the kind invite," said the weary knight.

The supper they shared was quite a delight.

Sir Henry then said, "I've written a poem I wish to recite."

Thanks for the company on this cool night.

Your warming fire is quite bright.

I say to you with all my might, thank you for being so polite.

Rhyming Riddle

What do you call it when you get hungry on an airplane?

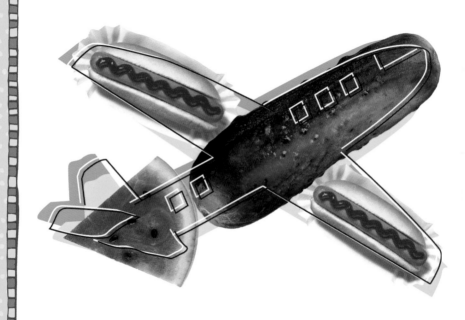

Flight appetite

Glossary

appetite. a desire for or enjoyment of
   something, especially food

campsite. an area where people sleep in
   tents and build fires for warmth and
   cooking

knight. a chess piece usually shaped like a
   horse head; a medieval warrior who wore
   armor and fought on horseback

pawn. the smallest, least valued chess piece

polite. having good manners or showing
   consideration for others

recite. to read aloud or repeat from
   memory in public

About SandCastle™

A professional team of educators, reading specialists, and content developers created the SandCastle™ series to support young readers as they develop reading skills and strategies and increase their general knowledge. The SandCastle™ series has four levels that correspond to early literacy development in young children. The levels are provided to help teachers and parents select the appropriate books for young readers.

Emerging Readers
(no flags)

Beginning Readers
(1 flag)

Transitional Readers
(2 flags)

Fluent Readers
(3 flags)

These levels are meant only as a guide. All levels are subject to change.

ABDO
Publishing Company

To see a complete list of SandCastle™ books and other nonfiction titles from ABDO Publishing Company, visit www.abdopub.com or contact us at:
4940 Viking Drive, Edina, Minnesota 55435 • 1-800-800-1312 • fax: 1-952-831-1632